Aesop's Fables

The Hare and the Tortoise

One day the hare is talking to his friends.
'I'm a very good runner,' he says. 'I can run very fast.
I can run faster than all the animals in the forest.'
'Really?' says his friend, the rabbit.
'Of course,' says the hare. 'In the forest there are rabbits, foxes, deer, badgers, beavers, mice, hedgehogs, snails and insects. And they're all slower than me! I'm the fastest animal in the forest!'
'Don't forget me,' says the tortoise.
'You!' says the hare. 'You can't run! You're the slowest animal in the forest! You're slower than a snail!'
'If you want, we can have a race,' says the tortoise.

'What! You and I have a race?' says the hare.

'Yes, you and I,' says the tortoise.

'OK,' says the hare. 'We can have a race at three o'clock this afternoon!'

All the animals are very excited.

'You must come and see the race,' say the badgers to the beavers.

4

'You must come and see the race,' say the mice to the foxes.

'You must come and see the race,' say the snails to the insects.

'Everyone must come and see the race!' say the hedgehogs.

It's three o'clock. It's time for the race!

'One, two, three… GO!' says the badger.

The hare runs ahead very quickly. The other animals can't see him. He's in the forest!

The tortoise walks, slowly but surely.

The hare can't see the tortoise.

'He's so slow! I can stop and wait for him,' says the hare.

The hare sits down under a big tree and waits for the tortoise. And… he goes to sleep!

The tortoise walks, slowly but surely. He passes the sleeping hare.

The hare sleeps and sleeps. The tortoise walks and walks. Soon he can see the finishing line! 'Look! Here comes the tortoise!' say the animals. The hare wakes up, but it's too late! The tortoise is the winner!

'Well done! Well done!' shout all the animals. 'The tortoise is the winner! Well done!'

'Yes,' says the tortoise. 'Slowly but surely – that's how to win a race!'

The Lion and the Mouse

It's a sunny day in the jungle. Some mice are playing and a big lion is sleeping in the sun.

One mouse jumps on the lion's leg. The lion wakes up and he roars.

ROAR!

He puts his paw on the mouse's tail and opens his mouth. He wants to eat the mouse!

'Squeak! Squeak! I'm very sorry,' says the mouse. 'Please, don't eat me!'

'OK,' says the lion. 'I'm a kind lion. Go and play with your friends.'

'Oh! Thank you!' says the mouse. 'Perhaps one day I can help you.'

'I don't think a little mouse can help a big lion!' says the lion.

The next day the mouse is walking in the jungle and he hears a roar.

ROAR! ROAR!! ROAR!!!

It's the lion. He's in a trap!

'I can help you,' says the mouse.

'How can you help me?' says the lion. 'You're only a little mouse.'

The mouse sits on the lion's head. He starts to gnaw at the rope. He gnaws and he gnaws and he gnaws.

Suddenly the rope breaks and the lion is free.

'Thank you, little mouse,' says the lion. 'You're a good friend.'

'Yes,' says the mouse. 'Little friends can be great friends!'

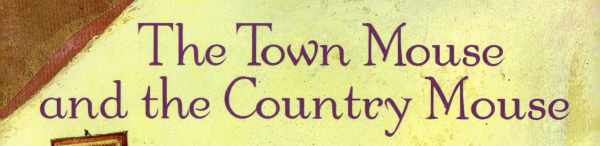

The Town Mouse and the Country Mouse

One day a town mouse goes to visit her friend in the country. The town mouse likes the fields, the river, the flowers and the trees.

The country mouse lives in a lovely little house. There's a lot of fruit: apples, pears and oranges. And there are vegetables and bread and cheese, too.

'The country is very beautiful, but it's very quiet,' says the town mouse. 'And I don't like eating fruit and vegetables and bread and cheese every day. I want to go back to the town. You can come with me. You can see what delicious food we have!'

The two little mice arrive in town the next day.
'Come into the dining room. We can have lunch,' says the town mouse.
The country mouse is amazed at the food on the table.
Suddenly, a man and a lady come into the dining room.
'Quickly, run!' shouts the town mouse. 'We must hide!'
The mice hide inside a vase. The man and the lady have lunch and go away.

'It's OK now,' says the town mouse. 'Now we can have our lunch.'

'This house is dangerous!' says the country mouse.

'Come here,' says the town mouse, 'and have some roast beef. It's delicious! Then have some chocolate cake and ice cream. It's all delicious!'

That evening the two mice
see a delicious fish on the table. But a
big, fat cat comes into the dining room.

'Quickly, run!' shouts the town mouse. 'We must hide!'
The mice hide behind the arm of an armchair. The cat
can't see them and goes away.

'It's OK now,' says the town mouse. 'Now we can have
our dinner.'

But it isn't OK! All the family — the man, the lady and
two children — come into the dining room.

'Quickly, run!' shouts the town mouse. 'We must hide!'

The mice hide behind the arm of the armchair
again. The family have dinner and go away.
'It's OK now,' says the town mouse. 'Now we
can have our dinner.'

'No, it's not OK now! It's **not** OK!' says the country mouse. 'I don't want dinner! I don't like hiding from the cat. And I don't like hiding from the family. I don't like this dangerous house!'

The country mouse goes out of the house. 'Goodbye! I'm going home,' she says. 'I like eating fruit and vegetables and bread and cheese in my quiet little house in the country. I don't like eating roast beef, fish, chocolate cake and ice cream in a dangerous house in the town! Goodbye!'

1 Read the sentences and tick (✓) T (true) or F (false).

T   F

The Hare and the Tortoise

1 The race finishes at 3 o'clock.   ☐ ☑

2 The hare sleeps under a tree.   ☑ ☐

3 The hare is the winner of the race.   ☐ ☑

4 Quickly – that's how to win a race!   ☐ ☑

The Lion and the Mouse

5 The mice are playing in the grass.   ☑ ☐

6 The lion eats the mouse.   ☐ ☑

7 The mouse helps the lion.   ☑ ☐

8 Little friends can be great friends!   ☑ ☐

The Town Mouse and the Country Mouse

9 The town mouse likes eating bread and cheese every day.   ☑ ☐

10 The cat hides from the mice.   ☐ ☑

11 The mice don't eat the fish.   ☑ ☐

12 The country mouse doesn't like the town.   ☑ ☐

The Hare and the Tortoise

2 Write the names of the animals. There are some letters to help you!

3 Write 'slower than' or 'faster than'.

A train is _faster than_ a tractor.

1 A Mini is _slower than_ a Ferrari.

2 A snail is _slower than_ a leopard.

3 An aeroplane is _faster than_ a helicopter.

4 A motorbike is _faster than_ a bicycle.

5 A footballer is _faster than_ a golfer.

The Lion and the Mouse

4 **Find the fruit! Write one word in sentences 1 to 6. What fruit is in the circles?**

1 There are two animals in the story: a lion and a
mouse .

2 The lion doesn't squeak. He __ROARS__ !

3 A lion's foot is a _____ .

4 The _____ is caught in a trap.

5 The little mouse _____ the rope.

6 The _____ breaks.

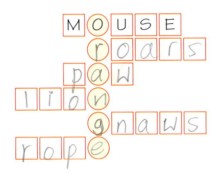

M O U S E
r o a r s
p a w
l i o n
g n a w s
r o p e

5 **Can you find these words in the grid?**

~~jungle~~ ~~lion~~ ~~mouse~~ ~~roar~~ ~~paw~~ ~~tail~~

~~squeak~~ **trap** ~~gnaw~~ ~~rope~~ ~~friend~~ ~~help~~

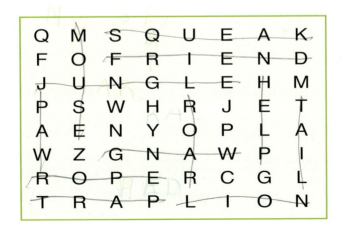

Q	M	S	Q	U	E	A	K
F	O	F	R	I	E	N	D
J	U	N	G	L	E	H	M
P	S	W	H	R	J	E	T
A	E	N	Y	O	P	L	A
W	Z	G	N	A	W	P	I
R	O	P	E	R	C	G	L
T	R	A	P	L	I	O	N

The Town Mouse and the Country Mouse

6 Look at the two examples in the story. Read the story. Write one word next to the pictures.

One day Tommy the **1** .... goes to

his friend's **2** .... in the country.

They take some food and have a picnic

near the **3** ....

A big **4** .... sees the two

5 ....

'That cat is dangerous,' says Tommy.

Tommy and his friend hide behind a **6** ....

The cat can't see them, and he eats their

7 .... and **8** ....

What is a good name for this story? Tick one box.

☐ A Happy Day at the River

☐ The Picnic

☐ Tommy and his Town Friends

7 Cut out the animals and put them in the correct empty spaces in the Sudoku!

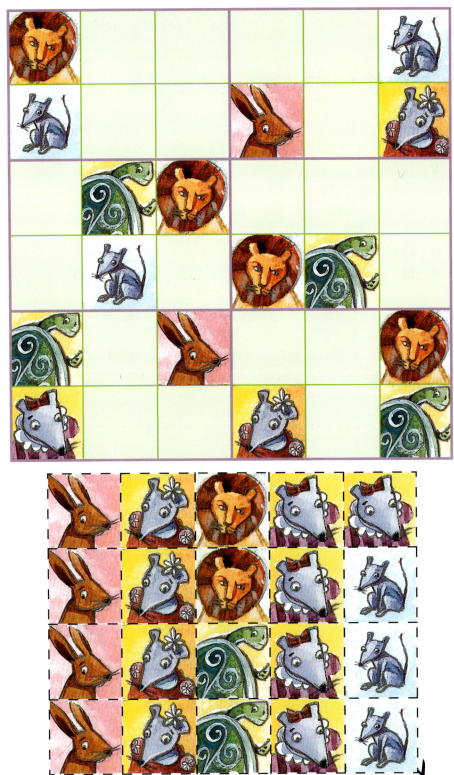

8 Match the letters A, B, C, D, E and F to the numbers 1-24. Write the sentence.

A	**1** !	**2** '	**3** t	**4** h
B	**5** N	**6** g	**7** A	**8** .
C	**9** p	**10** a	**11** l	**12** c
D	**13** d	**14** l	**15** o	**16** r
E	**17** b	**18** s	**19** e	**20** i
F	**21** w	**22** E	**23** F	**24** n

1 **B5 = N + D15 = o + F21 = w**   N+o+w = Now

2 **D14** _____

3 **C12 – C10 – F24** _____

4 **D16 – E19 – C10 – D13** _____

5 **A3 – A4 – D16 – E19 – E19** _____

6 **D15 – F23** _____

7 **B7 – E19 – E18 – D15 – C9 – A2 – E18**

_____

8 **F23 – C10 – E17 – C11 – E19 – E18** _____

9 **E20 – F24** _____

10 **F22 – F24 – B6 – C11 – E20 – E18 – A4 – A1**

_____

Now _____

_____

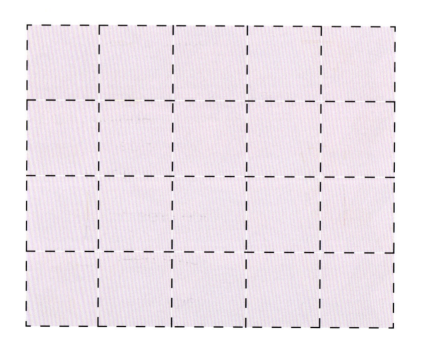

Picture Dictionary

eat :

go to sleep :

gnaw :

help :   hide :

jump :   play :

run :   shout :

sit down :

stop :

wake up :

walk :

finishing line :

race :

win :   winner :

dining room :

table :

armchair :   vase :

bread :   cheese :

chocolate cake :

fish :

fruit :

apples :

pears :

oranges :

ice cream :

roast beef :

vegetables :

country :

field :

forest :

jungle :

river :

town :

rabbit :    snail :

tortoise :

head :

leg :   mouth :

paw :    tail :

delicious :

quiet :

dangerous :

beautiful :

badger :   beaver :

deer :    fox :

hare :   hedgehog :

insect :   lion :

fast :   slow :

behind :

mouse and mice :

inside :   on :

30

Key

Activity 1:
The Hare and the Tortoise: **1** F; **2** T; **3** F; **4** F.
The Lion and the Mouse: **5** T; **6** F; **7** T; **8** T.
The Town Mouse and the Country Mouse: **9** F; **10** F; **11** T; **12** T.

Activity 2:

Activity 3: **1** slower than; **2** slower than; **3** faster than; **4** faster than; **5** faster than.

Activity 4: The fruit is an ORANGE.

Activity 5:

Activity 6: A good title is: The Picnic.

Activity 7:

For instructions on how to play sudoku, visit our website: www.blackcat-cideb.com

Activity 8: Now I can read three of Aesop's Fables in English!

31

Editor: Robert Hill

Design and art direction: Nadia Maestri

Computer graphics: Simona Corniola

© 2006   Black Cat Publishing,
           an imprint of Cideb Editrice, Genoa, Canterbury

First edition : April 2006

We would be happy to receive your comments and suggestions,
and give you any other information concerning our material.
editorial@blackcat-cideb.com
www.blackcat-cideb.com / www.cideb.it

CISQ CISQCERT
TEXTBOOKS AND
TEACHING MATERIALS
The quality of the publisher's
design, production and sales processes has
been certified to the standard of
UNI EN ISO 9001

ISBN 978-88-530-0511-3   Book

Printed in Italy by Litoprint, Genoa